CW00547126

Sarments

Sarments
New & Selected Poems

John James

Shearsman Books

First published in the United Kingdom in 2018 by
Shearsman Books
50 Westons Hill Drive
Emersons Green
BRISTOL
BS16 7DF

Shearsman Books Ltd Registered Office
30–31 St. James Place, Mangotsfield, Bristol BS16 9JB
(this address not for correspondence)

www.shearsman.com

ISBN 978-1-84861-578-6

Copyright © John James, 2002, 2011, 2012, 2018.

The right of John James to be identified as the author
of this work has been asserted by him in accordance with the
Copyrights, Designs and Patents Act of 1988.
All rights reserved.

COVER

Every effort has been made to trace the copyright holder for the cover image
and obtain permission to reproduce it. Please contact the publisher with any
enquiries or any information relating to this image or the rights holder.

Contents

New & Uncollected Poems

Selected Poems

Author's Note

'Affection' first appeared in *Shearsman* magazine; my thanks to Kelvin Corcoran & Tony Frazer. 'Romsey, Take 2' first appeared in *Tears in the Fence*; my thanks to David Caddy. 'Rouen' & 'Sketches from a Bristol Palette' first appeared in *Zone*; my thanks to Katherine Peddie & Eleanor Perry. 'Flickering Encounter' first appeared in *The Wolf*; my thanks to James Byrne. 'The Appearances, 'From the Welsh', & 'The Night' first appeared in *Poetry Wales*; my thanks to Nia Davies. 'Vocalise' first appeared in *A Screw in the Shoe*; my thanks to Lou Rowan. 'The Green Ray' first appeared in *No Prizes*; my thanks to Ian Heames.

'The River' was commissioned by JocJonJosch to mark the launch of their project & exhibition *Worstward Ho* & read at the Orange Dot Gallery 4 October 2013. It subsequently appeared in *Hand In Foot*, the catalogue for their exhibition at Musée d'art du Valais, Sion, CH, in celebration of their award of the Prix Manor 2013; my thanks to JocJonJosch, Rye Dag Holmboe & Jo Melvin.

'On Reading J.H. Prynne's *Sub Songs*' first appeared as the livre d'artiste with lino cuts by Bruce Mclean, designed & produced by Bridget Heal with the support of Ivor Heal at Queen of The Dart Press, Ashburton, 2016; my thanks to Bruce, Bridget & Ivor.

I am grateful to Andrew Taylor for discovering the fugitive poem 'Nightmare'.

From 'Poem Beginning with a Line of Andrew Crozier' to 'Recollection Ode: Les Sarments' inclusive are works selected from *Cloud Breaking Sun* (Old Hunstanton: Oystercatcher Press 2012); my thanks to Peter Hughes. Of these, 'A Visitation' first appeared in *Tears in the Fence*; my thanks again to David Caddy.

From 'En Sevrage' to 'Last Days of The Vulcan' inclusive are works selected from *In Romsey Town* (Cambridge: Equipage 2011); my thanks to Rod Mengham.

From '6:00 p.m.' to 'Colonial Medley' inclusive are works selected from *Collected Poems* (Applecross, WA, & Cambridge: Salt Publishing 2002); my thanks to Chris Hamilton-Emery & John Kinsella.

For the present volume I would like to express my grateful thanks to Tony Frazer not least for his support & commitment, his diligence & extraordinary attention to detail.

New & Uncollected Poems

Affection

one does not work out of a reaction against but rather
out of affection for something
                    —Barry Flanagan

I

guide my soul to the light from this unwholesome pit
where all is sold for an arm & a leg the stirrup pump
to no avail against the incendiary hail as countless children
hunger for tallow calling from faraway cities while radios
drone on masking the salacious trembling hand to fist
a sardine can almost fast food who wants it now
got no other option the drudgery of minimum wage
or listed in the Sunday supplement bought in the family visit
to the super store with mum & dad & baby buggy large as life
what do they want they do not know until they find the box
American breakfast with green top milk & loads of sugar
shake so nose to the ground the lengthy strap that pulls the dog
so careless like its human chancers show every piercing
& tattoo as yomping down the aisle they go no bended knee
or supplicant incense bow aroma of aftershave will do no
blessing now required as nothing told but enter pin code now
the 4x4 awaits as shriven by the carwash men as cheap as that
a quickie without the smokeless public bar the little town
not quite a capital spot to try for pollination
a double bed can wait

2

Fruiting bodies vintage
garment by the carpet pile grandpa full of what he's led to believe
some stinking rubbish from the daily junk adorning flaccid
regular the mat falling on us all as the queen lacks semen
popping drones following the soak of neonicotinoid
what good are they well there's munitions
pull up his joggers crossing the road against the red
two fingers to the horn the camera can only lie in shaky grey
by what stretch can this be called an art house cinema
our visions of grown up fillum lacking schedule
would you credit it best to buy your olive oil from Aldi
at least in winter bare flesh concealed from blatant view
dot & carry at the ankle loss of pace in sorry state
wrapt in a shiny body warmer Soviet black felt scarf & woolly bonnet
seeking something good to eat to take home to your kitchen
forlorn sell out of the local to the multiple estate

3

                      Bite off the
top of the morning on the high road to the bank no froth
or gain to see the pitiful junky lost to the world beside the path
would you believe it yes it is there tension of neck muscle
can't wait to get back home make fast the door rewind
the dread & disarray of the street to climb the stair
to application love of the creatures seen from the window
at the secrétaire you will continue till you ache the line
will turn & turn again in ascending barometric pressure
before you rest to reconsider what is done a draft
a pattern showing how it's made

4

        Call-sign freedom
of the kitchen taking the bird in hand & spatchcock for the grill
a little pile of carrot slices layered in the pot for Vichy
mortared pepper bursting aroma of the juniper under your nose
man on a roll a glutton for more throw in a soupçon of garlic
pursued as Norah showed you by the glowing range so long ago
toiling in the back of the house away from traffic noise at the front
she's standing on the stair again calling your name faithful as ever
in spite of everything hot on the hob a quick sip of red
a drop to ease the perspiration dripping from your brow
another splash of southern red brought in from Carignan
Napoleonic Guards are marching on back Rod Steiger at their head
a marvellous recreation but the deadly Prussian cavalry in black
infest the possibility stifle the scenario of the struggle
all was lost but now we have to stay alive to get things done
to wish for calm & certitude resist the pelting rain
that drives us to the lee of the house flicker of
painful surrender denied

5

   land of the free
TV direction what cost dominant intrusion severed our conversation
broken linkage in the aftermath of 1953 soon to be washing whiter
without blue or so she thought American all over as the hotter prospect
spinning like a running dog & working for the Yankee dollar
removal of hedgerow not recorded in the broken archive
never had it so Macmillan said but why should we always tag along behind
as in a chaingang with mist shrouding the forgotten garden shelter
corrugated pile encased in turf like a charcoal burner bonfire
arms slung over the swaying washing line you play in your bonnet
sheets of glass breaking your volunteer fall in the blink of an eye
take off your socks to feel the pain of shard extraction from your leg
feathered deep in gore a flowing dream of torture worse to come
in Castlereagh heart beating for the ravening constable any old tale will do
then back to your cell would you believe it take it or leave it in your
   own time
one finger one thumb keep talking swear by Almighty God the whole
   shebang
still breathing with a bloody mark on anglo conscience
no further questions asked each man & woman spoken for as beast

6

                    In the curving
surface of the screen the news today a baleful pornographic dance
defies your sofa plump up the cushions skip the ads
the Devil now assails your weary visage
but you say Hail Mary to send him away that's what we do
say no to all his works & pomps deny send back his penetrating gaze
flick the switch tear up the card & cross your legs before the fire
of celebrity eating their way through muck before your faltering hearth
listen to what I say or speak your own sequential prayer
zap each shadowy intrusion & abide the possibility of better times
break off & rearrange your own interior without external guide
that deed of stolen thought it's beaten out of you to cut you down to size
it's take you over time in substitute Weetabix a catch phrase or two
rises in your throat you'd better believe it they want you to swallow it
proceed to eat your Horlicks in the darkened room a spark of light
in the fallen log ash before the power supply gets too expensive
cut down the cost entailed inside the home renew your Senior Railcard
drink deep from history ancient story modem pain unheimlich durance
but for a moment recall all that was not lost in the guarded outlook
of our cherished circle our careful ambience in these four walls
en garde my love a hoard of peace & happiness in time abundant
though worn out by work & visits to the doctor never cost a penny
even when strapped for cash we never lost for thought

7

        All right core rescue
a discount buy one get one free there must be a snag what choice
their sale no goods exchanged sharp elbow mob at the bolted doors
employment some privilege measured by proportional leisure
poor judgement a hazard for the unsuspecting fail to hear the tinkling keys
unwanted stock is what they queue for it's in there ready for the punters
stripped to the limit of a store card an afterthought too late
back at a northern high rise on the forgotten edge of town without a prayer
with the digital radio on now chosen over daytime telly the smelly dog
        assents
still us the object of the exercise broadband quicker than ever so watch
        yourself
though remember where you began free nuclear attack advice
that was in advance of the multiple consumer choice of piercing
debase what beauty for a *Hello* colour promo weeping wound
a surplus over youthful skin a guarantee of future anal witness
mastication before expectoration superseded by no legal aid
a cost removed by further difficult decision

Entire violation

unnatural condition of the current privation
all in it together club armchairs for some subscription fully paid
but must we succumb what can you do they say
lie down for it under the cosh & boot acceptance
a last defence of '83 now long forgotten the People's
March for Jobs Saint Paul what was it you wrote regarding women
Mary Magdalen of Sainte-Baume you'd never credit what has now become

9

Coda: Salut

he appears in my dream
in the glow of his thirtieth year

clad in robes of
blue & gold satin

smiling he approaches
the orchard in winter
sickle in hand

Romsey, Take 1

it's calmer crossing the railway bridge
at six o'clock in the afternoon in late July

as weary stragglers hasten home
heads down at the end of another working day

no trains to speak of
the traffic thinner now

the sky suffused with soft white cloud
& arcing screamers

linger a while beneath the maidenhair
outside the florist

the deer at rest in the thicket
over at Barnwell

& the blackbird sings
cerebral cerebral

Romsey, Take 2

the prions are in everything now
including the flies that you eat
as you walk down the street

but above the ridge tiles
a thrush is chanting
those who love have hope to bring

the slate is not so dark
though beauties you have few
but cherish those you do

it's Saturday & the Bohemian proletariat
gather at The Empress at six thirty sharp
the talk is of a Portuguese departure

as the blackbird sings
Virilio Virilio

Romsey, Take 3

the tree of heaven
reaches for the sky
beside the Council depot

beside the railway bridge
alive with rooks
in the prelude to evening

it's the hour of the apero
& weary workers
head for home

a latchlifter
at the tavern
before dinner

of a Monday
the bar so tranquil
but the craic will fly

& the blackbird sings
Mauresmo Mauresmo

Sketches from a Bristol Palette

but then again the '50s never really went away
                                        —David Lynch

i

it's Saturday night in The Quinton
Percy Wilson shining black hair en brosse
immaculate black drape white cutaway collar
black knitted Jacques Fath tie
brown dark-banded eyes ready for havoc

ii

Alan Cottrell in The Somerset
squire on leave from duties of protection
telling the story of the Battle of Sedgemoor
embellished with grace notes from Villon

at every rhine weapons of sickle & scythe
oppose the leaping cavalry of the King

Cottrell's hidden arms of Toledo folding steel
rattle in their secret straps in the lining of his trench coat
as Don O'Toole on his night off from The Old Vic
separated from Alan in the confusion of the evening

searches for his cigarettes on all fours in the darkness
of the front garden of a house in Worcester Road
under the watchful eye of the Constabulary

iii

Big K— from Jamaica
leaves his collection of Louis Jordan
in our care
while he serves time in Horfield

iv

Little K— from Trinidad
is out of town again
leaving an attaché case of dynamite
beneath his single bed at B—'s

soon he'll be back with fivers for us all

v

waking on a bench in The Centre
early on a summer morning
the placards tell us Billie Holiday is dead

Flickering Encounter

after Bataille

He is standing, a crypto-interrogation, his lisping voice modulated with an exaggerated elegance, like Brian Sewell. I lose track of what he's saying as soon as he's moved on. Something about money. I've heard it all before. His centre parting, cigarette & insinuating frothy teeth. His lips merge with his drawn face while his motionless half-folded arms & taut shoulders endorse the damp temperature & neutral decor of the fading country house. Why do I even consent to be here? Why can't I simply leave, motor down the gravel drive, not even slam the door behind me? I'm dazed with the emptiness of the occasion. Leaning forward in a commodious armchair, she listens with a glinting attentive gaze, her hand holding a glass of mediocre sherry. She colludes with the intrusive questions of her stepfather. In this sordid yellow light, as the church bells toll in the valley below, I am, if for this evening only, one of the defeated.

The River

for JocJonJosch

the Taff agleam now
with the rolling flanks
of sunlit trout

& gushing
through the Vale
beside the City

beside the Castle
beside the Feeder
the western boundary

of old Newtown
the once Irish quarter
at the dockhead

o navigator navigator
so many canals
& rivers in this island corner

of the archipelago
all points of the compass
leading the way

for us to wander
the holy Severn
the Bristol Avon mud

the little Cam in Somerset
amid the green covering of
coalfield & slag

the slow sullen Cam
at Silver Street Bridge
where swimmers leap

& The Old West River
pulsing on into the wide flat range
of the rich black fen in winter

so tenuous in mist
with the lunging flight
of a mighty heron

breaking away
across the narrow channel
of a dark lode

or out from Lechlade
on to Greenwich
under the spatter of

industrial chrome yellow
over the Thames
passing the Mudchute drifting slow

* * *

free from the clamps
& straps of the yard
cast off from its oily berth

without a sail
the wooden coracle emerges
three Jacks aboard

the rise & fall of each light oar
pulling away
in round negotiation

the tainted light
of the mooring
trailing behind

afloat with
each trembling oar
outstretched

revolving without a bow
in a swollen current
travelling on

going with the flow
via the little drop
through a sombre thicket

adorable streams
arise under trembling oaks
trickle down

through narrow channels
to the bank
a paper cup gone west

some broken rail fence
leaning down
to the water

where Friesian cattle
drink amongst the
sinuous river weed

the early morning light
shining on their flanks
as if by Cuyp

long green tresses
sway in the current
a hint of rain

delicate droplets
in the hairs
of each sailor's head

passing beneath an arch
descending from lock to lock
body object & river interact

& diverse particles
flow slowly on
to the furthest margin

reflections on shifting water
the sycamores aflutter
in pale anticipation

fall of protective
willow branches in early spring
the river not so cold

a deep pool
where a salmon
lies resting

perhaps a light rain
filling the vessel
but survey

the interior of the heavens
the lowering thunder
drifting in

* * *

pipe up boatswain
that patch of blue
may be the sea

sand martins give way
to marine breezes
& Stripey Goss

at the width
of the river's mouth
a curling wave flows out

the surface glints
an ebb tide running
under soft grey light

the shoals break up
at low tide
& carried toward

the indelible horizon
three oarsmen striving
in rotation

driftwood & foam
crunch the wild wet shingle
yielding to breaker

but we're with Brendan
seeking the island
what anchorage to find

Un rêve du soir

for Philip Crozier

They shuffle slowly forward on the pavement in a broken line extending some thirty metres from the Metro entrance. Their clothes are dark or russet under the cadmium orange lamplight. It's mild for later winter, dark already, but the sky is touched with cobalt blue above the blackness of the buildings. A shop assistant whose little son & daughter wait for her at home with mamie. A nun without her veil in subfusc civvies & a beautiful Muslim girl in a green hijab on her way home from the Lycée. A carpenter in his hi vis yellow jacket & whose wife has recently detached herself after twenty years determines to be resolute. I worked on this all day wanting to show it them before they'd gone. But it's not ready yet.

Rouen

your strength stems from working in the fields
the gentle calves caress your face as you lay
resting in the embrace of aromatic summertime
a fair haired girl with a touch of red
enchanted by the choir of nightingales just as later
the distant Angelus bells their sound
stealing across the little hills entrance you
with the thrill in the air when they stop
& the voice of Michael calling in the cattle

The Appearances

in the midst of all that shrieks & roars
shellfish speak other of churning hearts
the invisible cliff to be avoided
but not forgotten what calm to be found
as a captive of England a cold country
in which to earn a living

on crossing the Pont her ashes melt like snow on
the surface of the swirling blackness of the Seine

later in Brussels I become your follower Marcel
in the winter garden amongst the palms
in the promesse du bonheur

From the Welsh

the bees arrive from paradise
laden with heavenly grace
so it is fitting that we burn candles at Mass

the wax the honey the mead
are blessings from these creatures
which flourish sometimes swarming
from their bellying hive of hardened clay
dancing in the trail of the scouts
that lead them from the lighting board
in the south east heat & light of August

we salute them with bragot
our humble glasses glinting in the sun

oh nothing is hidden from your courage Siân
while herding in the tender calves
sun's parching heat deflected
from your face by the broad brim
of a straw hat of all base passions
fear is much the worst

Sunday Afternoon on the Esplanade

this place has something of the sacred heimat
a screen flickering rich with elaborate memories
quickens the beating heart
under the old platanes under La Marianne
the seniors rest in the shade

failing the oral chemistry test
we caught it from Brother Francis
leftie rightie for the strap

but there's no going back to what was there
your streets & alleys & your father's hat are gone
your old school torn down the church
where you were baptised engulfed
by the glassy towers of Babylon

fumes overpower the little bench on the corner
at the crossroads where you took your break

it's 2:00 p.m. in the clear blue heat of summer
after Muscat on ice & caracoles the hour of the sieste

take the same route o passenger

Vocalise

Ich leb' allein in meinem Himmel,
in meinem Lieben, in meinem Lied!
—Friedrich Rückert

from cutting shapes
clouds disappear

it's 6:45 p.m.
at La Manière

a sip of Fontcaude
before dinner

the stars will soon arrive
above the courtyard

beneath their gaze
take a pill for pollen

it'll be a
long long time

before the night's
over tonight

& two logs
don't make a light

The Green Ray

I

after Tacita Dean

the horizon drawn crisp & clear at the edge of the world
where a giant sun slowly descends
some hundreds of miles away in a dry air
chance of a later green after red & yellow
an offering sought but elusive up to the last
where it may appear as a splash as the sun departs
in a processed reel of film it is there
caught in the flickering gap between frames
in the face of digital proliferation
a material defiance seeing is believing
& it is there

2

after Robert Desnos

between the scope of the tragedy & the charm of the night
the trees in the forest clatter alarmingly
legendary creatures are hidden in its density

at night insomniac footsteps echo those of the prowler
the phantom constable the orange glow of the street light
& the early totter's lamp

the trains pass in the near distance
as do the boats on the Canal
the last cries of the tawny owl at the first frisson of dawn
& you are there

a practice scale on a piano & a voice breaks out
a door slams & a clock chimes
so many creatures & objects & their sounds

but still there is the quest without end
there is you the one who is anticipated

at other times strange hypnagogic figures appear
at the moment of dropping off & they vanish
a hundred phosphorescent blossoms fading

beautiful intelligencer there is no doubt you are there
with your steadfast soul tangible & expansive

like the sweet aroma in the air the stars the crowing cockerel
the cry of the peacock in the park lands
in a blaze of kisses
you are there

hands clasp each other in pallid light
creaking axles on trance inducing tracks

you are surely there nothing can say otherwise
persistent & leaving us guessing on waking

as the crow flies over the abandoned power station
where concrete beams perish under a leaden sun

you are the root of dreams & free the spirit from its multiplicity
leaving your simple glove at a kiss

in the night there are the stars & the sea's dark movement
the estuary, the little town, weeds, the lungs of others
there is sleep & there is you

3

after John Skoog

we sense it is late on earth
between the hour of the dog & the fox
the Swedish farmer strengthens further
the outlying barn with random lumps of metal
grey cast concrete beams & outstretched girders
corroding in an atmosphere of fear a vibration from afar
a mighty army far out beyond the horizon
sending a series of unnerving bow waves
to the edge of the shore & never otherwise appearing
but in the encircling dusk the barn is slowly there

Waza-Ari!

the black redstart
devours
the fallen olive

The Night

reading John Wieners in the old house at Ross Street
lamplit corner pages on an evening late in '86
the door bell rang & Jeremy was there the book set aside
where were you that night? Catford?
a Black Sparrow in hand again years later
after reading John Temple's *Scarlet Shadows, Lucent Shade*
a gift from Wallonia in a spacious room in Hertfordshire

all is devoured & connections made unto
the current fragments a scene with so much now
subsumed by an academy of new blood
a cut away from the Bohemian decades of
Wieners Bristol Better Books Lee Harwood's smile
& Andrew supping bitter in The Rising Sun at Eltham
a community of intelligence shared across the mouths of rivers

but now all is cut away from the base the Thames
the sea the coal the steel the ships the docks at Cardiff
John Callaghan at 16 walking home from work on Planet Street
stripped from the reel by a relentless ascendant decay
numb anti-climactic flash of a hundred cameras
reflections in a shiny black door on a day in early May
tomorrow gridlock Cambridge sprawling beyond limits

9 May 2015

Alphaville '58

remembering Veronica Planton

on the corner of Berwick Street
hair the sheen of blue steel

& legs in 12 inch
lemon yellow jeans

a vision after Cappuccino
at Sam Widges

we recover from the fatigue
of Bratby & the Beaux Arts

as if on a wrap around veranda
the Zulu War Song in our heads

accompanied by thoughts
of Billy Cotton

we're wide awake
in Soho

heading for Doug Dobell's
to see what's new from Riverside

I do my
Alain Delon

she says
linger Watson linger

& we do later
in The Nucleus

on Monmouth Street
the gloves hanging

fingers down
above our heads

Cork City Manifest

clouds of Mexican fleabane pink & white
adorn the stone-clad banks of the River Lee
its double channels complicate your route
in the fatigue of vagabond flânerie

intimations of Seán Lucy Patrick Galvin
linger with a pint of Beamish at An Spailpín
as mother called you when you misbehaved

in '47 the ancestors began to exit Skibbereen
sailing as human ballast out of Cork
to land as wetbacks on Glamorgan shores
to labour trimming coal at Cardiff Docks
the women cleaning in the great department stores
for fine Edwardian ladies who shop & lunch

but now a feed of bacon cabbage spuds & parsley sauce
then climb to Shandon say hello to Trevor Joyce

A Sonnet

for Ian Heames

autumn arrives early when you least expect it
a touch here a touch there
& you're tipped into the prelude to winter

strange aromas blow in from The Fens
& there's that Cambridge hum again at night
in the darkness the head frets on the pillow
a low frequency drone testing anxiety
rising & falling at around 36Hz

is it a government protocol or the roots of trees
the chestnuts have had enough for months
eaten alive by the leaf-miner moth
turning them red as the burning oaks of
ancient Cymru or the glow nocturnal over Hotwells
as Bristol now affords a buzz of Western savour

Solid Elements

for Ian Patterson

thin lines of rain slant down
on shining roofs of slate in Splott
a Japanese wood-block print effect

walking to the shop for sherbet lemons
keep the change for going Maggie said
the flagstone pavement leading straight ahead

black pools of sludge build up from GKN
wet trellis gardens quiet of a Sunday afternoon

the stony edges of each terrace
angled firm against the south-west breeze

Gregorian chant drifting over from Saint Alban's
a fantastic occurrence like anti-gravity
a solitary bicycle hissing by in the road
& bread & butter inches thick for tea

Sanctus

for Michael Grant

towards the end of May the day of Saint Joan
the girls in the fields with the calves look up
& see the silver dawn just as they remember Reims
we too were dancing on the side of a hill like them

but in the autumn we must attend the earth
where the weeds are seek & feed desire
to make it new discover balm for the hurt
that time inflicts to thrive on the hope
found in the brilliance of youth & held secure
to greet the teeming gift of days with elevated cup

On Reading J.H. Prynne's *Sub Songs*

'As Mouth Blindness'

her low voice beguiles me
amid the tumultuous foul

eases my head
in sleep at night

otherwise the road unrolls itself
a machine in the penny arcade

on Brighton Pier
whoever said the going was easy

but we have no fear
the stars gradually emerge

in the royal blue trapezium
above the court

the purple wine
my broken chair

nothing more now
nothing left to say

'Creosote Damping'

the dépendance
certainly needs attention

the shutters won
against the sun

the fingers fever
at the clavier

unseen
Jean-le-Blanc

hangs on a thermal
above the garrigue

somehow lit from below
like a cloud

so sip later later
when it's cooler

prune the pêcher
in November

I adore
encore

'In Forge Incremental'

oh we shall see
all right
if we are spared

the blue & yellow birds
swoop together
from the cables

each to
her target
& me to mine

under the vast
blue of heaven
seldom silent

day to day
on delta wing
they have it made

'Riding Fine Off'

the hen harrier
glides low

over the garrigue
female

driving into town
for lunch

more coffee
the day's

requirements
sufficient

otherwise it's
non non

& again non
to all your worldly goods

we stay at home
to write

dare to wear
the onyx ring

me too

'Accept on Probate'

cut the bread
with the sharp knife

in the glow of the midi
for lunch for

a morçeau of Salers
for the sangliers

it's the opening
of the season

the hot swain
tastes the cool wine

fill but not
to the brim

what is the burden
of your song

love without end
amen

'These Nothing Like'

clear away
al fresco lunch

finish the coffee
& read the text again

below the sun's
reflected glory

hand held out
to show no blade

thinking from the top
house martin

not yet gone
skimming by

carrying love
in its heart

the Lirou rich ochre
after Sunday's storm

the trout upstream
fins beating to stay on course

walk on
indignant as ever

take this fig from
the arcing branch

'Thus to Look'

fast to work
the bliss of writing

in the early
part of the day's

unfolding hope
before the rush

of other business
intervenes

then the road home
lit from above

by the generous sun
in late afternoon

a posse of quail
scatter fast on foot

before the advancing car
slow in the bloom of day

'Skim for Either One'

do this now
& not in vain

before the green
is parched

by summer's end
an August storm

might yet alarm
the pine

though bonded to
the stony earth

as we to each other
lip to lip

& limb to limb
toiling back to back

the trail rising
to the pass

the mountain air
pushes at the window

cooling the room
a shift of focus

'Along the Wall'

yes one to one
interior with silent writing

cooler space
behind the wall

no parity
of coinage

in this trace
step by step

our hands held
side to side

in the face
of everything

the rain held off
the roller slips from the wire

skimming blue
over the vines

Nightmare

blots of heat
start from the perfumed head

o my sad red shadow
under the stairs where your iron feet clatter

I watch you pass through a chequer-board of shadows
easing the hammer to go

your destiny flaps
a coat in the wind

the flies buzz & a profound somnolence overcomes me
in the heat of this cucumber frame.

It's the bullet for you
& your superior brand of manic didacticism –

these hateful overtures
are less than a pleasure

the egotistical assassin
boring away at his unhappy victims

who accept as it were
an erotic boon.

People pretend to like it
& whoop it up by the churchload

a public spectacle of garrulous proportions
his degenerate appearance

is a carnival event
relentless as a piccolo

he presses before himself
a revolted sense of shame

but his star is on the wane
like the smile in a vigilant mouth

a monstrous image rises in
the calcified glass of his eye

this is the truth which breaks out from behind
a grinning hand

let's have a little resilience to all this sweat
my race-going friends

all those tongue-tied vowels
immobilised against the rails.

Selected Poems

Poem Beginning with a Line of Andrew Crozier

of this, see, she returns on tentative bloody feet
into the light offer of hope shed by the sun
a protective skein or do I mean skin which warms to its touch
even as I speak of you thinking of Jean
with a glass of wine & a loaf of bread as
a cloud passes over & our smiles fade for a moment
then return as after lunch we talk things over
with no idle word

I reach toward the poetry of kindred
where we speak in our work as we seldom do otherwise
from memory cancel the dark impatient for the next poem
the afternoon afloat the garden of song thrush & blackbird in May
the sun agleam again on the aerial pole above the ridge
cancels the cloud & so to the shed
light the moontiger reach for the hoe
to mark the narrative in earth

or walking home at six in the evening after work
along with all the others flowing over the bridge
thinking of you & all you others
writing alone with the radio on

at the kitchen table I put a hand to my breast in sorrow
then reach for the wine still singing
& your book resonant of a life
neither following nor in pursuit
at the end of a line let me read it again
staying awake it is a dream before birth to dream anew
of this, look, diolch & again diolch

A Visitation

driving through softer light south of the Thames
in March the gorse in yellow flower on Ashdown Forest
where lovers kiss in summer time among the bushes

check-in complete the engine cools & the glass flows over
supping alone for tonight on Harveys Best in the Lewes Arms
where once a diva called to slake a thirst in aid of opera

now clerics dispute the way to write the time so out of joint
as far away the rushing air beyond the Severn
rocks the tolling bell beyond Nash Point

a child on the shore scrambles over blue cobbles
looking up to the light above the bivouac in the clearing
before coal slate farm & quarry close

& now a darker figure hunches home against the rain
oh Simone o sea moan

Breakfast at Red Lodge

Stop on the Turnpike in the month of May
& after breakfast head up country. From here on, says J,
grinning over a serious forkful of Red Lodge Special,
we're in the Texas of East Anglia.
Is that so, says J, with mock sobriety.

The counter of the cafe painted cheerful red, the tea is hot & brown
& the heads of passing saints smile down
from the wall on these two pilgrims
laughing madly in the Hopper window
where space opens up into the blue beyond the red & white stripe canopy.

Years later swirls of sandy dust blow low across the truck park over the street.
At the next table Asterix the Gaul steadies himself above a dish of red meat.
HGV men return their empty plates & are gone.
It's a sunny afternoon. Drive on, they say, drive on.

Reading Barry & Guillaume in Puisserguier

the sun is splitting the azur above the garrigue
as I settle in the corner of the courtyard
in the white resin chair
in the shade of the pêcher
reading of horses boiled in blood

thousands left their homes for the rolling lands of the north
for the Trimdon Grange explosion
the shells falling at Asquillies & Verdun
Mrs Burnett & Norah Hart both lost their sons
& now our Danny rests in peace at Langemark

this evening my darling Pat has taken a bise de soleil
& retires early so I go down to the Café des Arts
to meet Peter Finn on the terrace
to discuss Auger Gaillard & his practice
& the gras libre & other matter

the craic of Oc is all around
tractors with trailers full of grapes are rumbling down the boulevard
Maeve's brother Joe turns up with his daughter & husband with busted
          cheville
on their way back from Croatia to the West Contree
so the talk turns to statues of James Joyce & numeric boxes

in the heat of the night I dreamt we were all at the *I Love You Poem Award*
at a reading organised by some hard edge dudes from the Later Cambridge
          School
they asked you to stand up
you were wearing a gorgeous indigo mohair suit
with narrow lapels made in Soho in the '60s

you received an ovation from the crowd
all seated on the ground

they took the prize away from Carol Ann Duffy
& awarded it to you
but you were not there

I had been asked to read by the beautiful Karlien & Lucy
but I leave my spectacles in the breast pocket of my coat
hanging at the back of the venue
I read the last poem anyway & improvise
before I close the book with a coup d'émotion

Barry & Guillaume I love your poems

John avot
28/29 août 2009

August

it was on the feast of Saint Christophe
we were looking for the house of René Char
with sketch map & books from the kind vendeuse

driving out of the Isle
we enter the flickering shade of the avenue of planes
but somehow leaving the river
we miss the route for Saumane
climbing instead into the Luberon
rushing odour of mad red wine & aromatics
arriving in the village of Lacoste
in the brilliant light of the midi

on the terrace of the little café
under the towering blocks of the Château
a barman in a white apron approaches
the purple wine is poured
at the next table an older man
with tawny wide brimmed hat
speaks to us in the tongue of his pays
we only half infer what is said
unsure of what we found there that afternoon

October

I'm meeting Tim at Millers at 6:00 p.m.
the hearth will glow the ale will flow
the banter will be light & fancy
later we'll go on to Jeremy's rooms
& take a generous glass of Glenmorangie

but the daily calendar pages flicker over
the talk turns serious
the trees are burning red
the moon is fleeting through the pallid skies
the Cam glides dark & sullenly below
the hearth cools in the face of the distant future

yet the lid of the box was lifted
it smelt of wet dust after rain
I think it was called hope

Recollection Ode: Les Sarments

as August counts itself out
like a Rosary worn with kisses
autumn arrives when you least expect it

cool in the tranquil morning light
before the washing of the streets in Béziers
recall waiting for the Barrow Gurney bus

recall those in prison & the sick
grey phantoms of Horfield & Haslar falling away
like a wet *Echo*

sorrow in the jeopardy of Jericho
Mater Dolorosa El Suspiro del Moro
Martin Godfrey locked in by the system in Tottenham or Knowle West

in Anglia young men look away in the face of age
anguish of low frequency noise at night in Cambridge
the unthinking arrogance of a petit-bourgeois on the make

a particular ostentation of car & cufflink
why is it always *Tosca* on the radio
the grip of March a prison set for days the dark blow

withering the grass as it hacks in
over The Sperrins to the north of Stewartstown
the cattle turn their backs

bloody Mozart the tabby from next door
crashes over the wall into the solitude of my soirée
excited chromium atoms emit a photon

falling to the floor
Ferlinghetti gets bent in half in Stockwell
thoughts gone adrift go west again

by the banks of Lough Neagh at Ardboe
where a trout lay singing
those who love must also hope

approach the lustrous water in the bath with care
be sure to keep the bolt on
lest all the demon Kirsties haunt your reverie

meditate the Mystery of The Three Amandas
lap-dissolve to Burton Redman Donohoe
by March the almond blossom almost done

but the base chalk works on the shot silk lining
a cricket pavilion shapes up like
a cinema in the woods at evening

a vision painfully acute
streaming before my very eyes
a close-up of early Rachel Weisz

the perfect manners of a peasant
or a vrai aristo
chips tonight rain tomorrow

set the brass repoussé table from Alex with Forget-me-nots
I like to think of Marcus on his yacht
The Beagle a dog I haven't got

heading out to Jack's Hill with Andrew
J's tie a strip of orange on white
beneath a crumpled grin above a mug of strong hot tea

the caff on the back road to Cromer
eating la salicorne des marais
the splash of le ragondin at Auch

I was a child when those white hunters ran at me
out of the dark interior of a repair shop
I was never afraid of dogs again

so I will haul these vines around for the sigh of heaven's kiss

o mon lecteur ma lectrice may you live your life
as on the wide part of the road with
no fringe or border to mercy

I wish you the fruits of the four seasons
& every day as the sun beckons
may you be delivered to that daily glow

En Sevrage

in the barn the lambs were bleating all night long
but beloved have no fear
at least they will not do so in their poetry

August 1996

Meet Your Friends at the Still & Sugarloaf

the peace of Ross Street on a Bank Holiday Monday morning
surpasseth understanding the rain serene
soaking the blue pitch of the slate roof opposite

under bland skies a grey opacity as of
milk in a bottle after a restless night
the phantom call of le petit-duc
from over the vacant sidings

the purple pavement hidden for a moment
the radio turned down low in the other room

reading an old avant-garde magazine
which seems to have been written entirely by one person

but it's wonderful to wake up & know that
despite everything
France is still there

so it's a little blue T-shirt day today
liver spots fade to freckles
& Jackson Pollock spits from the heights of Mount Olympus
into the broken teeth of Hobson's Conduit

you play beautifully but there's always someone who will deny you
that's why there's a certain tension in the wafer area
the telephone obdurate as ever

but if as in a dream the stars caress the soul
as once a youth swimming in Poole Harbour
the neutral buoyancy the pure & tainted empty light
brighten the pages of Laforgue
as you lay on the roof of the cabin
reading in the sun

make no mistake about it
what you were looking for was already there

At Château Chinon

le pollen c'est l'élément mâle de la fleur
le Morvan like a house of granite
south of Vézelay a fountain
so much the work of de Saint Phalle
a festive figure play of gold
a giant hand with golden fingers tipped in red
& overall the arching twisting jets
turned on by a kind of local boy
who became a great president of France
unlike some grinning simpleton back home
in thrall to wealth & glamour & celebrity
& at what cost

in fact never trust a body builder
or men with legs like Indian clubs below their baggy shorts
or any seriously stupid people
you never can tell what they are going to do next like
take up an Italian gangster or invasive surgery
any one for martial arts he lisped

but on the trail of La Boucle de La Chapelle
close by Our Lady of the Oak the spring rises at our pilgrim feet

or on the boulevard de la République
your happy smile protected by a parasol

a petite woman in black
pays tribute to a little sparrow
& the people are captivated

so why in this moment of well-being should we want to see England again
that overcrowded space become a fen of half-occult corruption
in state academy & civic hall
all trust eroded failing system & due process

manners & liberty lost to abandon
more windows soon to close again in claustrophobic places
soon to be shivering under sleet & snow & hail
each word of art as a good in itself an irritation to the mighty
what hope of greater joy for those at the base of this monstrous tower
as the rich get richer with parental choice

but we have to say goodbye to our daily bread dear heart
go back to where the sessile oaks are valued less
& even monumental trees decay

sure then Brendan we'll be steadfast & depart & travel on
seeking the island cheerful as can be
such lowly duties on ourselves again to lay

Baudelaire at Cébazan

your text is traced in burnt sienna
across the span of ochre wall in the old Co-op at Cébazan
& tells me now as it did in my youth
of how the wine sings in the bottles
of the toil & poverty to come of deprivation
calling out to all the honest people of the earth

but even in its glass & vermilion capsule of lead
the wine offers up a song full of light & solidarity to those
who know the solitude between the vines in winter
who know how much it takes on the blazing hillside
who know recurring trouble sweat & pain & the burning sun
bringing to life the vision of their hope not full of hate
but flushed with delight in the throat of a man worn out by work at
          the end of the day
knees under the table deeply reassured & breathing quietly
content to raise a glass he looks into the smiling eyes of his companion
as the echo of the Angelus beats out the song
a little girl is singing in the road outside
weariness falls away at each fresh vegetable sip
something precious returns like a seed cast again
& reaches toward the heavens like this scarce flower

Nocturne with Baudelaire

a singular glance
slipping toward you

a white ray
flicker of moonlight

loose change
on the bedside table

kiss of abandon
warm skin beneath the silk

late in the night
with Françoise Hardy

2004 & a cry of pain
in the street outside

all of that
all of that

the wine to hand
wild thyme on the hillside

balm to the palate
& thirsty heart

pour again hope
la primeur

& pride
the virtue of the work

restore to us an inkling
of the sacred

A Touch

the sky is vast today
& we may ride
with no restraint
in rare clear light
together

caught on a rising breath
as though the sea itself
spoke to us here
so far inland
of harmony & desire
borne up by
natural grace

Pimlico

we're going to be late for Jackson
elder blooming softly white in darker green
arising from the soil beside the railway track
but we do eventually enter the temple of light
craving beauty

strange how seldom you see old friends at the Tate
but I saw *The Deep* at the Pompidou with Andrew & Jean
sat down in a lavender mist in Washington DC & had no doubt
no doubt that you were beautiful beside me
no doubt that you are with me in the world again today
& a passionate exhalation hangs before my eyes

you do get a higher standard of beauty in such places
the tiny scar on the brow of a boy
an Asian eyelash

I don't buy a mousepad
but I do choose some postcards before we step out into the sunlight
where a young man in a green sweatshirt
is seated on the lower steps amongst the crowd
an even better looking Andrew Duncan
reading *Capital* the mystery of the fetish

you were the youngest boy
& the paths lead & the feet follow
pointing the direction of the future without arriving there completely

a slipping glimpse
like blue remembering green

                    Gulnaz gliding towards me
                    in her hijab
                    on booted feet

a black V8 Pilot
on Bruton Place

& another
concealed in the name of her veil
with blue steel hair

& 12 inch lemon
yellow jeans

figures in Green Park
linger in crafted nature

& stepping from this parting
collapse with fatigue in The Morpeth Arms
a borderless community & haptic private silence
turning the Sapolin loose
Richard walking in the grass
Andrew walking on the grass

& I took flatness as my starting point
the line made quicker in its shorter pulse
& slower in its flooded length

the line a slinger to the surface from the depths of things
where a breath touches the slightest branch
& bends the stuff of accident to your will

shadows of tripod & camera
Neil Henderson in the lower right hand corner of the frame
a print come through

I lost the beginning of the thread
as Ariadne said but nothing was ever the same to begin with
the airplane the bomb & the radio on

the tears wept the sweat broke
the paths lead & the feet follow

our ancestors visit us in dreams
God don't

Last Days of the Vulcan

seeking anchorage in marshland at the margin of the city
pace beneath the railway bridge space opens out the gate
to Adamsdown before the gradient earth of Splott
grey swirls of rain & soot above the shiny blue-slate roofs of Ellen Street

beyond the viewpoint of the Upper Sixth on Courtenay Road
flames pour up the fading pallor of the evening sky
as Brother Columban offers eventide of gems at 3 o'clock
& dogged boys & men squeezed dry of acid reach with aching arms

cross the old footbridge for foaming amber sleeves
a flickering interior of older bearded men caps laid aside
this orange glow holds out where a thousand sparkled on a vein of steel
the sigh of the oppressed fades into luminous indigo outside
backdrop of rising corporate towers canicule & sweat are spoken of
in lapping voice & the flying arrow turns away from lively warmth

6:00 p.m.

Oh, CALYPSO
CAFE ESPRESSO
Charlotte Street, Clifton
last of the old 50s bars
in this quarter

with your decor of plaster masks
as detached as
the faces of your clientele who
stare at them
& the red roughcast walls
sectioned by bamboo uprights

or through the window at
the evening streets,
the pale stone octagonal
of University Tower
discretely presiding over
the nearer façades of
ladies' dress shops.

Ο, Καλυψω
we're all waiting quietly here
in that interim
before night
really begins.

The Postcard Sonata

I

so, awkward lazy & indifferent,
I mooch along no tiredness left.
Under gigantic limbs of trees, the air's
persistent pressure cloys at
the skin as damp as steam & light,
tawny as amber, drools slowly by.
The whole flat range of the tenuous fens
may even trickle with it

over the horizon's precipice. If I continue
on my hands the pain I carry
in my legs may die, fading to nothing as
the scattered galaxies & nebulae
merge from their nascent places in the
endless drifts of evening sky.

2

for Andrew Crozier

Fluff, grit, various royal deceit de nos jours
began coming home to us in 1967 Andrew,
visiting the Borough gallery in Camden, eyes
blank with the dream of our cock-eyed dreams
the dawn thing suddenly isn't tenuous
admiring Peter Cartwright's *One Two Three
Four* & *Five* all menacingly fluid but
precise, a relationship between the formal

& the unpredictable. Later driving away
with a friend who'd deserted his wife
a journey of sickness on his sleeve,
they saw the outer lights of the city
a fabulous gold collar agleam
& liked those careful graduations also

Forty

with Andrew Crozier

I walk along, left so alone,
indifferent, lazy, the gigantic limbs
of awkward trees – indifferent to
persistent pressure of the air
as damp as steam. Light cloys
translucent amber beads that
dangle from uncluttered weeds as
sinuous as living breasts that quietly
swell from tenuous ground
no tiredness left: so awkward
under banks of cloud that threaten
rain the way is shown to
wards a London where the sun
is rising & we meet again.

4

Wormed & rusty like a quarried fox
her memory dreams of tower window stars

          Such brutes!   apparelled

in a brilliant seething rush of nothing to hear.
So she fidgets,
concealed in the name of her veil
with her gunbarrel hair
& bunches of stubby fingers in the frost

Mugs of black widow!   is the
cry as I go into her, but lost
though feeling her cream: it's cold & hard
on little purple hearts. But that was years ago
& now through window-bars "The blue night sky
her basement memory dreams

5

Receding to views from the western boudoir
friends & old women refrain to step out in the slight
acridity. Later, these hags are poised precariously,
conscious & pleased! – ohh earthbound planets
glare on kerbside still rosettes!
Police-cape rainy streets are soaking all tonight
whether they creep alone or sleeping together

under the steam & pressure of
monstrous artificial skies –
vituperated, loathed, & longing to blaze away
at flickering eyes between the slats

That cold commemorative tale the unforgetful past
is thrashing about in a pail of our freshly drawn fears.

6

The elms' gigantic limbs, mild soft cheese
& pickles in the rain. The slight facts of the case
were terribly venomous to him,
shining through barer branches
like the sky as the season changes
like that soft starry "you"
& the tawny sky receding westward
where the stars will soon appear

in distant space that stretches deeply out
beyond our grasp, sinuous
as riverweed in the rain, as her hair
in the swollen current, oh madam we
receive but what we give
"weak, slothful, a voracious reader"

7

Whatever "this vague outline of it all…
afloat on the watery air, a clutter of
little zoomy puffs
                    That old song of crickets
dissolving into fields
her burning vacuous brow,
such pallid events
I'm unable to read any more

owing to optical difficulties –
the palimpsest kind,
quite often met on station platforms
so late at night & crying
                              on account of the northerly air

The lovely face of Edith Scob

7a

She had this
                    dimness

falling all day long, like the
quiet distance of hills

& a fiery arc of
coruscating hair
                    made up a
frail screen for her
vast green stare

& the stars will soon appear in this poem
like a politic image

like little hopeless words

like sinuous river-hair &

endless drifting
evening sky

(coda)

A recurring condition of the frenzied
                                        is fatigue
                        & I lurch a bit
                    passing out of a Purcell
                    concert.
                                    That torrid elegance
                        is abandoned as I
                    pass into a week of
                        prize-winning beer which is also
                a week of concurrence in
                        self-abnegation, dappled
                    with tiny shadows
                                        cast by
                        unrepresentative events
                        I'm unable to read anymore. What?
Quelle furie! – What drizzly days before the season
opens up on us, new & original as a diary
                under the rusty nibs &
                    blackened blades: "…a
            sinister appearance in doorways, an arc of
                    fiery hair, sa robe de soie
                    un brillant rouge
                                        turning/

            to the tune of 'Pannonica'

Letters from Sarah

I

from time to time that which is resilient in me
retreats to more jaundiced hideaways
or I hang from a hollow tree
waiting to be cut down by a travelling lawman
who later turns out to be a bounty-hunter
or a soldier from the muddy lowlands
draws back the curtains of the bed
as somebody turns on the fountain

my little girl is standing out there in the courtyard
the hotel wardrobe as empty as my head

tell me slowly now
the shoals tremble & break up at low tide
when do you want to leave
your passport your intentions
the bridge has been destroyed by dynamite
the screws are on their way

the heavy black painting in the corner
which piece to move which lamp to choose for your pleasure
this autumn of burnt documents

I love you your quiet features in the glass
we're leaving little one
it's calmer on the island now

we display ourselves like an order of archangels
under a fusillade of white bullets

2

at the frontier we gave 'em a lot of madam
before accelerating away
to an accompaniment of whistle-blasts
into the forest a breather under the beeches
our hands & faces black with ink
the roe-deer were eating nuts or something

I got your letter & in reply to your question
I can only say that I know he already loves you etc

at the dockyard we pick up a lot of cheap bananas
there are hoists for the animals
the sails bulge as we walk by
our new secretary is a simple creature & is going out
with a right collection of villains free of charge

but this living to repeatedly break off
can one speak of the soul as a sort of inward draught?

the sky turns a brilliant yellow in the late afternoon
a devilish irritation breaks out between the fingers

I've only myself to blame for this syntactical vocation
balancing, one finger on a bottle

3

how have you lived there
without a goat
some hens

in the sunny courtyard
the king dreams away his exile
standing by the well
or walks in the vegetable garden
throwing pebbles at the
grasshoppers

the sun goes down pulling with it the last of the open sky

put the flowers in a proper vase
& place them near your bed

4

an incredibly gymnastic sniff
can give me a thrill
as does the jutting forth of your arrogant breasts
& all my years lead up to this like twists of straw
I hope to have that waltz with you when I return
& watch our bitterly clear reflections
whirling in the mirrors of the hall
o listen my love that morning in the hills of the interior
I was a deity of no importance
or a humming-bird
or a chimney-sweep
or a servant girl in pain
my mistakes are clear to me as are the crossings-out
in a very long letter
one receives in hospital
you comb your hair so conscientiously
& when I dash into the chasm for my medicine
pursued by an hysterical pack of stylists
you become as insignificant as a false passport

5

the afternoon streets were all velocity & rage of steel
but in the steadiness of seven o'clock
steam is rising soothingly
around the glass of this continual departure
which brings down fatigue in a vertical arc
& wraps the heart in an old newspaper

so the song is colder now
& I'm wearing the resonance of black
& silken embellishments to lay against the skin

how very great it would be to see you again
with shining limbs spread out like scissors
carving up memory into garden shapes
but the whistle blows   :   partons

always the same direction
the distance always expanding

6

I light a cigarette & watch the ducks in the park
the keeper's calling in the boats
reluctantly the evening lights come blinking on

on the other balcony
someone looks away
the hotel violinist starts to play

they're lighting the candles in the dining-room
the flames spread out
like a fleet in formation.

The ferns are seeding the plains of my destiny
snowing under certain pieces of reckless foolishness

7

the way you put out your fingers wavering like your eyes
this warm restraint
if you were here where my hand slides under the cover
the shops are closing
the little girls are going home along the street
soon they'll be absorbed into the shiny sides of buses

under this resonant ceiling
I wish you a cooler breeze
like a sleepless vault
or a cleansing
& the quick leap of vowels
I repeat:
the gale under the trees   the little church   those looks
of yours
which measure the depths of something

but come let's avoid the particular by invention
a seasonal appeal to your frailty & arms

there are shafts under the mountains
& my lungs are wakeful as a trainload of Tottenham supporters
midgets for beer & madness

8

the fever & obscurity of our organisms
the matchless flowers of

in the snow of the interior

only touch me
& I'm brittle as a snail-shell
at the edge of this broad white country
all colourless wind & poplars

who gives a damn anyway
drooly girls with blue umbrellas
are bombing along the slide

drops of ink the flowery envelope

9

so lay yourself closer to the earth
& learn the secrets of iron & wine
this shapeless land will never coalesce
though wads of snow fatten the mountains
the dark roads soften to cheese

& in the spaces between the peaks
thin rays of light will turn
like the spokes of a bicycle wheel

10

(i)
teeth like yellow gravel
dance on the stem of your pipe

(ii)
some oppressively physical sounds
from room 27

(iii)
pipe composure

(iv)
why don't we take the road for Cologne?

(v)
in my brainpan
some abbreviated ideas
like button mushrooms

II

Benjamin leaves his chair & walks up the hill
moving neither his idea of himself
nor the hill
nor the shackled man
nor the old tram-lines
sunk in the tarmac
understanding only the line of parked cars
he means nothing other than himself
a pair of legs walking on marble
throws away in the street
what he no longer needs

does he put out his language
or is he soothed by a star
as he tears out his tongue
in the last part of winter?

the hemisphere tilts
the second version of the year begins
as hair & nails turn down

12

as the stars
zip by last night

I learn something new about you
paper friend

making a call in
the wings

you fly away to where there are
streams to adore

& sheep aspire
to your royal favour

13

"pass the salt & then the wine

the diesels howl in the night
while we in secret dine..."

the candles flare up in the draught

he was quite dead, his face
firmly planted in the pine needles

wearing the same old overcoat

illuminated by torchlight
the pale flight of an owl
decorated the ceiling

the adverse wind
rattling the weathercocks

the bandage yellowing on my arm

14

hey lanky one
in your double mask
come near me of your own accord
with tired limbs
your opinions of no special importance
& ambiguous blue blood

when you stand in front of my head
cool your gratuitous desire

trail yourself over this couch for a while
& enjoy the tainted light
which floats up from the harbour

later we'll set out again

15

don't turn your head & colour when you
glance my way your smile
as though you ate the sun for breakfast

sleep when you're tired put me away
between the two long lines that hold you tight
the cable cars the heights
you'll want to fish those glacier streams

there's an old char
smelling as clean as a chemist's shop
a white-painted house
& cereals
spooky flutes
that play at night

stay horizontal
if you wish to go there

16

we will go, clouds
to the Falkland Isles
arriving like Skotch Mist
over the crepuscules
we'll shade the hills a darker green

Goodbye little dress-shop boys & girls,
an affirmation passes with us
like a morning frost in June

leaving the oaktrees to their doom
an almanac in each of them

for the snow
to melt into the earth of mountains

watching for dawn
in an oppressive bedroom
all that water piped away & into fountains
in the municipal squares

wanting the dawn
though a wavering moment in the dark
may hold something at least
that may last, though you can't always see

what it is you appear to want. Well,

oblivion finally is extended
whether in the occasional insouciance of sleep
or to the sacredly drunken it settles
over the dusty pavements

       & then the little birds fall upwards
       & across the sky
       from chimney to chimney

& among the folds
of clean white table linen
the glasses are poured & waiting redly

       so das strömende Wort
       the onrushing
     may still be granted & holy
      remembrance also
     nothing'll be forgotten
    either tomorrow
        or by night

the day writhes in an immense crater
some gleams want to burst out now & then
but further off on the taut horizon
the wind moves hardly at all it becomes
necessary to wait for the voices to return I
put down the pen get up & fasten all the doors

& soon the painted gauze descends once more
it looks like you again but with the centrepiece mislaid
the parti-walls tilt back revealing the greater sky
where a star comes loose & a shadow runs over
everything closes up on itself a
single occasion in the time continually piling up
but when will I be able to come to the moment
when it's possible to finish everything & begin again
you never look at me when will you be able to come back

it's only a game but oh so steadfast we keep on
passing the brink of an elegant nothing though
sometimes something in us makes everything tremble
& then the world doesn't exist anymore
or else we're mistaken & it merely makes a different sound

then it's yourself you see behind the universe
a dancing silhouette in a series of portraits
you fail to recognise any of them
but they're family you're looking at
in the middle of those motionless faces
the only one who's living is apparently the most placid
he leaves never to return

in the room where the walls are beginning to smile
it's only the night which gets up to leave
it's getting cold
your attention rises toward the stars

27 October 1969

for Barry Flanagan

There are some lights & we will name them, thus:-

    1, the flax & the wood

    2, the wood

& the flaxen arrow of

          your hair is shorter this afternoon
          a pale grey light at the back of your head

          & recently snipped
          a few tiny hairs

          little creases in the arms of your jacket

& in the top of the flax

              the one suspended
              curving fold

  a neat dark shirt
  no fuss
  perspicuous gaze
  walking out on a rainy pavement in Bern

  "hmmmm"

the rope demolishes its own presence

the rods

the tilting perspective of the wall
the white slightly scuffed where it joins the floor

the ominous corner

the panache of flax in air

polish

3 long sticks

Will the points?

right, not even paint

to a depth of three inches

Good Old Harry

we go to sleep like anybody else
though some awake like bullets
like Romans
munch munch

we aren't Romans
we aren't Americans either
we drink a lot of beer
every nation has its own greatness

we are the English
easy-going & lazy
we sleep pretty well
& when we wake

we are usually pretty thirsty
but not for anything too drastic
you can trust us to be
wooden & quietly proud

of our laver bread
our dumplings
a tomato or two
does no one any harm

& if there did happen to be a bullet amongst us
it would never find anywhere to go
it would just keep travelling through the air
without hitting anything

we have thirty-eight rulers
which is very economical
& they are well protected from
tomatoes on the whole

we call them the cabinet
& cupboard is the name of the land
where everything is in its place again
the natural rulers

behaving like proper gentlemen again
eating a bit of cabbage
& sausage now & then
like the rest of us no doubt

when Edward goes for a walk
we take off our caps & wave them in the air
England is a mature nation
& is not a bit like America

May Day Greetings 1971

eating a plate
from day to day
sharper than ever

blow your nose
in authentic
rigorousness

advance to bonheur

A Theory of Poetry

it's very important
to make your lines
bands of alternating colour
running from one side to the other

these will bind
your poem together
like an egg
& make it exist

a reticulated broken edge
the positive ingredients of
banality & repetitiveness preferable
to histrionic virtuosity on most occasions

indeed be dogged
it's better to be expressively dumb
than full of mediocre elegance
& bullshit

& though expensive paper will provide
the physicality your poem needs
you can also apply a bit of boot polish
to transparently tinted over-painting

& in this act of obliteration
performed in a fusion of
calculation cynicism & fervour
the poem will suddenly realize itself

this will subvert any/ deny any/ positive/negative
narrative reading
& stress the written surface
with all its openings windows apertures leaks

& the incongruity of this literalness & frivolity
will induce in the reader a greater objective awareness

reading is often a big help
but wherever you turn
you are surrounded by language
like the air

you will find the difficulty of working this way
makes you long to be

another kind of poet
however try to be stringent & lean
as well as luscious from time to time

assert the bodily means
by which your poem is written
after all
as the man said
thought
is in de mouf

standing out
luxuriant & mundane
against the subtlety of English light
which is the foil

you can afford to be less cerebral
less intellectual less brilliant less clever
less locked-up-in-your-room-at-night-ish
less reticent & deferential

& more programmed flatter
more all-over more environmental
always
on the prowl

for the materials
of your existence
in the city
which is sometimes what is meant by spirit

get as much as possible into
sitting-rooms bathrooms bedrooms
kitchens & hotels
gardens parks & streets & saloon bars

there you will discover
particular people at a particular time
& in a particular place
these people are the others
without whom you would not exist

avoid the countryside unless
you are going to do something there
like ascend Helvellyn
or shoot a brace of partridge to take back to your kitchen

useful activities include
eating talking & dancing
listening to music (preferably live bands
looking at paintings & undressing
dressing & undressing

do not be too overawed
by wide open spaces
love France by all means
but love your own language first

that way it will be of your own
as well as your own
& will be trusted by neighbours
& summer visitors alike

& thereby your formal relations
untempered by such vulgar considerations as taste
can adjoin
crude broken ridges

overlaid by sluggishly dragged bands of the drab & blaring
can adjoin
delicate smears & caresses
that

Inaugural Address

Good Day/you're in tune to If You're Going To Do It Do It
Alla Prima Time/

it's a Radio Babylon interference calling
a largesse of Delirius
more fundamental than America
ruddier than Silbury & more abused
greener than Mekonta &
mightier than the Wig in Wigan with a yellow in between/

Dreamier than the Kill in City
shinier than Krypton & more clear
more on top of it than Atlantis a
Blow Out on the Bauhaus
A Roll Over Old New Veau
A Knock Out on a Nico off the DD & D Co
A Granite Against Gropius/Toasting with The Hosting
No Touting for Bruno but
pouting & more tantalising than
Island Three the desiccated orifice of
The Woman with The Three of Everything she say
What on EARTH are Maltesers/what in THE WORLD
is a Power Tower/

A Cruising in a
3rd Century of The Decline
of Industrial Investment I & I for short The
Fantasia of The Plan Voisin Begat The Beaubourg
Glossier than La Ville Radieuse
& Sharper than Arcosanti The Architect
is The Invention of The Masterwork &
couldn't live without it/

Wrecking his Neck-Angle on the EuroStandard
we drift & mooch in the marinade of his metered Overspace
down on the Bogside Jesus & The Redevelopment Corporation
snicker into sight a fault in the beam-out from GPO Tower
back in Finance Capital/
neglected scabs of Venice Florence Rome Glasgow
flake under foot
on the black marble stairs of Milan Station

Inside The Riverside
Articulate Trace as Non-material form of Capital
blisters each side of your face with a blush
an intense blush blisters each side of your many faces
in the flux dance slab stance ba
lance of glittering felspar
the straitened moment speeding
in the ruinous curve of vinyl & circular dwelling
a cutting of deliberate gesture
in the passage of indelible act

Good-bye Savonarola Brunelleschi Alberti Bramante
Good-bye Dublin The Centre Pompidou The Guggenheim
Ghiberti's doors are the doors to the biggest bank
The Los Angeles County Museum of Modern Art The Hayward
The National Gallery "West" Berlin & Hello Tokyo
Good-bye the Monumental Fault & the Faulty Monumental
Great Fish-Knives of the Future Hello/Good-bye
Good-bye.you fully automated cities that keep operating after we have
        all left
Good-bye computers transistors space-probes automation miniaturization
        acid & San Francisco
Good-bye the Marlborough Good-bye Sir Humphrey Gilbert/
not a room to be had in all of Broadacre

though you may get there
on The Old Straight Track
By the Rights of Orthogonal Planning/
Good-bye Auschwitz Hello Angkor Vat Pol
Pot Napoleon III Pinochet Pinocchio of Chairman Hua
Haussmann Mussolini Sant'Elia The God
Father of High Tech & he with no lustre on his
bite in the echo chain of Sardis the thatcher the carter
Teheran the Arc of the Shah
The Biggest McDonald's Advertisement In The World
Whose Cancer spreads easier than butter Kissinger
Rockefeller The Woman With The Three of Everything
Everything Terminates The Wedding
With Frozen InterContinental Rice/
Miniaturization of the Social Body
Into Occasional Table Arrangement
Micro-Explosion of the Thousands Transformer of Millions
peripheralized to the slotted sides of the votive Gold Heap
Market of Commodity Futures Miniaturized orgasm
of little yellow men spray from the planet edges
one by one
we drink & eat the sweat
& muscular steaks of Africa straight from the freezer
on Microwave Alert for The Republic
Sparta Miletus Periclean Athens:
The Acropolis Metropolis Necropolis Death Star Voiding
Hearthstones into 3D Vision Gelatine/

C'mon EveryBody/let me take your little pinkie
point your knees overhear
see me in the Arkle light of me anti-perspective altar back
shift your gear over here
get your fore-quarters into tune
& put them on this here blue plinth
Before your very stereoscopic vision
skyjunction Sky Junction
flux in sky junction Masterwork the flux of/
This is Sky Junction

Craven Images

"Oy vay! Oy vay!"

I like to dance so much & a kind of mania
conspicuously lures me on to your pointed hairless chest
but since here I am engrossed in the reading
of this here copy of *Sounds* & I am not Mechthild
only the punter with his meat on fire
outside the station in the fog I will swear
never to have seen you before in my life
when the Old Bill cruise by on their talking machines
matelots linger at the cab-rank I
carefully flick my second finger over the hard &
shiny folded notes in my shirt pocket
as the lull at the end of a lonely street
in the orange glare of the vast suburban night
holds me to the sluggish rocks of the pavement
your face in the shadowy shopfront at 3:00 a.m.
ain't exactly the ski patrol but then what with this
disaster area called my teeth like a roar of jacks
in a flashing orange search for a burst water-main
among the indeterminate commodities at the corner of the bar
Jackie Petersen dreaming over his amber sleeve of Brains
one immaculate black hoof over the brass rail
under the falling cloud of resin & chalk
passing from night to desk & desk to night
shoulder to shoulder with an immaculate new fish-tail
Where are the hatters of Luton? American devices
come round again like a thousand Chinese paper inventions
I would have liked to have been to Bucharest with you
Budapest anywhere taken all the boats the wagons-lits
mooch round all the bars gawping at all the young dudes
ate up all the food making for the Man in the Moon

crossing the Park in the soft purr of taxis
ah that sweet viola sound

> *her back is arched*
> *& her breasts are bare*
> *I feel a rose down*
> *in her hair*

the inimitable life of hotels
a rich display of feminist cactus in the lobby
lingering crows on the steps of Brompton Oratory
the poor animal life of the region we
will try the grand gesture the sag-arsed manner
the sculptors throw cat & rip off cock manner
tails the piece the hands of me manner
& up to a certain point manner
a couple of borzois on a leash manner

> *o baby what*
> *a dog to be*
> *in the Suck Age*
> *of the bourgeoisie*

perhaps I could finally bring myself to leave
your baleful pluralism my fingers
pause deliciously over sticky keys
as I hover over a faint icy rhythm
straps vibrating under your immortal propositions ideal
pedestrian on the King's Road
enraptured by the stare & cheek of very early Logic
another little Pils & pointless artless & frank
I get drunk without you
until the mixture degenerates & a bad odour
returns us to the Angel the harp player of the age
scraping his knuckles on the rough-cast ceiling
blood on the tambourine I sing
under my breath & my you're nervous

under the snow of a cold algebraic desire
an inkling of a kiss in the foyer
but in the calm of your bed in the late afternoon
there are these agreements of the body
the little pores in your back the gently lifting slats
parts of the outer city are atrocious
hatred of the meagre portion
even the bars are closed when we leave the cinema
it never stops no end in sight
till morning takes you home
here is your bed
be stupid beast & sleep
last of the occupants
who sadly scrape their feet

2

in the lines of the slipstream of an heroic express
coming in on the long curve eastwards into Cardiff
Atlantic rockas make their move a brazen cloud of
fiery smoke is lifting over GKN as we embark

& in the palace of globes a dazzling array of glasses
 in various stages of depletion
& the sweet high tenor of the craic

under the rain under the sun & under the starry circus
the green sea rolling like an egg

3

black moleskin
tender pastures juniper & Coke

far from the underworld
green penetrates the sky levels

a glass of Volvic could have made me happy for ever

4

a glass of Avèze held me smiling vaguely in the grass
like a great lost wader
sad to have been a fighter & at what cost what times
& what a summer where are you now my little musics
mind you cowbells
                          make me sick
with misery & pain

                          '…twenty times I have denied my heart
                          I am no longer able to rest'

I flew far in pursuit of your traces
une peinture une musique qui serait simplement voyou
the insanity of my legs the millions of my thighs
the tang of the pike in the mouth
a piece of chocolate sweating in the sun
like a very rare stamp in the middle of a banal collection
the bosses vacate the City at the hour of the illuminations
thousands of voices lift themselves up to heaven
in a velvet liaison with her boulevards
like love among the ants
the strawberries were ripening my ideas were turning blonde
the sky glazes over the purified volcanoes

5

The west side of the fishpond in the Jardin des Tuileries, looking across it & down the long terrace to the crepuscular distances of the Place du Carrousel. It is a bright sunny day. The usual scatter of public chairs has been cleared so that only three remain & these are placed very formally in a row looking out over the water. The carp or whatever, are jumping about all over the place. It is August 1970. There are two figures sitting quite still their backs & heads quite strikingly neat & similar. But the one on the left is Arthur. The other one is Douglas. The chair to his right is empty. "It's high time I was getting back to England you know, Douglas."

6

I was leaving, love on the platform
possessed of your greatness, o dear Thames
windows all lit up & rosy in the setting sun

This morning at 10:00 the Inter-City 125
will float me to Birmingham Stoke-on-Trent
but at the eleventh hour you grow sick at the rumour in the back of
      the heart

likewise my craving for newsprint the smoke of small cigars
a proper slow burning characteristic of a superb condition
tumblers whirling downwards over shining rows of slate

your ideas were captivating & the wounds superb

as we rush out of Euston I turn & smile at the disappearing grass

a dart has pierced to the centre of this alluring folly

Bad Thoughts

"You are unable to imagine that one day it will be possible for
     you to say hello to yourself to recognize yourself as a
        friend & to make a definitive peace of that
you remain surrendered to your alternatives
when it comes to tomorrow you are unable to recognize yesterday

the defunct days lean towards you with their images
from them you read off the inscription of your old outrages
& those yet to come tremble away into distant complaints

the scattered griefs fail to gather in the vicinity of where your heart
     has been
you have forgotten why you are sad
but you will know the hour where your sadness was born

tired of searching the night you will relish the day
she will nourish you with her light orchards
the trees of the night the trees of the day

the seasons turn in their balmy cycle
& you will not know what to say to their mild passage
it's a big chance you think it over

you cease to see yourself as a fit up for what is agreeable
exhausted by the winding distance covered by your staggering days
the lost homelands the rusted autumns

     & a fiery rose in the September sun
you will feel your body give way to its constituent parts
it will bear less resemblance to you than a rose-bush
the spring lies in wait for in order to prune
when the evening twilight falls on the deserted lane
you will not have any dread left in you

you may wish to cut yourself off from certain parts which you
        disapprove of
you would take a slice of this thing or that to offer up as a quarry
but when you rest on the restful breast of your lover

by her let yourself be carried as far as the border
where to be cancelled itself is to revoke all endings
accept yourself & your heritage from which you have been formed &
        passed from age to age

stay mysterious rather than be pure accept your multifariousness your
        pluralism
when you come finally to take leave of your youth
all the fallen dreams born of your very early childhood

shoot beside fresh jasmine
an adorable person comes together in your arms
at the charming little cross-roads where the day slopes

into the flat open country & the little hill expires
the implicit beauty of sacred places will be troubled for you
this restlessness will have put everything in question

& you will be subject to the craziest actions
but the road runs away from under your step the horizon never
approaches
& you give yourself to this walking life to which the dust of the road
        attaches itself

Karol in Tunisia

1

Did he imagine the difficulties of the road he wanted to follow
when he was dreaming of his first compositions, when he was writing
operettas which he presented with the aid of his cousins in his
native village out on the huge Ukrainian steppes?

   A poetry of yellowing pages, the charm of the eyes of the young
Scriabin, a certain grace, a lightness of texture, there is no knowing
how his powers would have developed if it had not been for
the friends he made in Warsaw.

2

It is almost March again. I have the impression that some little
boxes with musical valves have opened inside me

      like a boy, a switch cut from the fields,
    striped matelot undershirt, white open collar,
       the air is moving the branches over my head,
     I am listening to its music, it

does not matter if from time to time some facetious &
   cynical little creature gives us a small bite
or that we are so seldom alone that instead of talking
   we make signs to each other

     the river glints a harmony
     sensitive, nervous & not invariably accurate,
     in Zakopane, there you can really be alone,
     wanting to be with friends, on the veranda,
     the double tones, the pasture bells,
     dancing a new mazurka

3

Before & long after Chopin there was a complete & prolonged silence. Oh Karol!

After Francis Amunatégui

The appearance
of a hot sausage
with its salad
of potatoes in oil
can leave nobody
indifferent...

it is pure, it
precludes
all sentimentality,
it is
the Truth

Bye Bye Blackbird

for Douglas Oliver

over the clay-laden estuary a
soft grey light comes sneaking
my heart away it is the spirit of Colne Spring

& all along the shoreline an oyster-catcher
dips & bobs a splashing blur of black & white
against the easterner

curlews ghosting by a little above the fleet
fly our souls out of perversity

Brightlingsea has grown where it is the sepia
gaff-rigged sails of the smacks manoeuvre away

into the Dutch hinterspace beyond Mersea Island a rich
alluvium gets itself laid over years we mooch along

towards a frith
dreaming of sprats & opals

Shakin All Over

dip your head in the basin & go
walking the early morning streets late March rotting
from the inside out leather under
dog-tooth green check tweed
lathering the aching in the rib-cage just got to be
got up & gone I'm not turning away I'm
not looking down I'm puzzling over
the influence of the Stickies I
freely enter your special unit I
don't look down
light drapes flap at the covered windows
touch at the hairs at the back of the hand
the shackling of trucks in the sidings rattle of
curtain rings & soon I hear that crazy fluttering sound
cut through an otherwise absolutely silent room
it's the undertones
of your vibration rattle of pink noise
the poise with which you set your arm alight
our mutual pride &
randomly chosen limited isolation

oh baby what a place to be to disregard
the giant hoard of wounds this tress
in the creaking of copper ear-rings
strands pins & hair-slides & drinking Black Bush
a wave of dark air rolls through the barley
& then you can recall it all &
jet discs rattle as you walk
close to the shifting metacentre
that stripe in your wrist where
the heat is still fresh &
reckless of the edge your face as pale as
quartz or gypsum you're turning backwards

to a new scene as the lozenge dissolves into
crossover & he leisters the jumping thigh
with whatever comes to hand a beer-can amber or zip
the flax caught in the teeth of the comb
& she cries out for once & for all
churning the mud in the pool

                              & later
in the studded augury of bar-tables in the Midland
the immediate future appears strictly female there
will be somebody to talk to & I like to look at you
without somebody watching over us happy &
glorious & even under close escort
the narrow band of pouncing
will be hidden in the skin
                         & we'll be
lapping up a sleek pony
eye rolling over a speckled back zigzag
the stun-shot sways you as you stay on top
they say you'll never be free
but give me your hand here
under the duress of sliding straps
the tang of the white bush
the linen spattered with honey & lager
the dawn spouting with little birds & pressing
a shoulder-blade to the mattress
& there's not so much as a bit of boiling pig
left to be eaten the coverlet hoods you
squinting into the sunlight the talk
twirls at your throat & your hard green
is painted with flashing white
emulsion disinfectant as you apply an orange
towel to the stomach the neck the
perforated magma warm & moist & groaning

Poem for Bruce McLean

"the carp in its dark pool
shadows the salmon of memory

under the feinting willow
their burnished scales

splashed by moon & stars
& violet petals

breaking through
these creatures turn

& arc in grace
against the blue

the rush of air
& flow of darkness

at the rim
the paler branches quiver

cascade lit
the mossy stone

& wavering lip
the silent fishes

turn again & glow
in long anticipation

as the veils of polythene are rent
in the temple

the canvas shudders
the flank of a horse

at the entry
the uncertain sky

so soon your eye will see the surface
in the depths of things

the rush of energy
& very early light of day

out of the cold of the lonely street
where the pain is dislodged
like an old triangle
in the field of the indeterminate
heads build to grey
modelled from single quick gestures of the hand the arm

the absolutely confident hand
tries out a few different pieces of body furniture

the green lips of certain women deny all appetite
as the hands of the others clench & point & smear

the mouth in the mirror receives its anointment
as the glass slides away
as the index signals 1

& the arrows of a bland libido
search out the goblets of a chunky wrist
the supremely confident hand chin attention
ways of arranging a boiled egg in its elegant cup
& I begin to know you as your luscious hair
drips into this containment

as your forehead turns into the room
obscures your eye in its elegant cup
a lick of red escapes me

the utterly direct basilisk stare
offset by the fact that one of its eyes
seeks out a third

so you give me touch sight & sound
the egg-cup becomes an ear-ring
& I feel happy again to be writing this

we live so much by the eye
but the ear's an organ too
which sticks out neatly from the side of your head
& carries an earnest of desire in the ring that dangles there

the left eye on her chin
the right eye swerved to take the light
that shines from his

the fish the triangular passage of despair
as the down stands on the nape of the small of your back

one eye on hers
the other swerved to take the light
that shines from his

over the heads at the pictures
that shafting silvery light is here again

softly smouldering postponable lust

the beam in your eye
the ever present assassin
the yellow lunula

like the bell signalling the start of another day at school
when we were very young & green

white man turning grey against the reds
above them the stars
the satellites the sausages
closer to home a tasty finger or a
knuckle sandwich
coming in from the side on a body swerve from somewhere else
the intruder in the arm of yourself
is it his arm or her arm or yourn
where shall I place this arm
not to put too fine a point upon it the fingernails
are edged in black right down to the flux link
the grip a little infirm as perhaps it should be
an envelope addressing itself
to the How Firm Handshake Question
keeping a careful eye on the studded wrist
your lovely breast adrip with paint beside itself

all this has been plunging forward through the week
the lamp burning in daylight

in the city
where your strong neck
merges with the line of your head
& your tough little mouth
very seldom falters

in the face of those other lips
which pose like satisfied anemones
those hands like gauntlets strike me
pink against that grey

but that'll be the day
a flicker of the country in the bar
blows in across the threshold of the open door
& your love was fairly near me too

oh probably on Sunday mornings as we lay in bed reading
the reviews & sipping cold coffee
even though it was moving off in the direction
in which it was always free floating

did you really think I'd ever stop

in the gallery your thoughts sometimes turn to such matters
as they do to cups of tea or chocolate rolls
which I never eat

but the writing's on the wall
you fill the width
before it suddenly takes off to reappear later
further down

by the set of their shoulders you shall know them
these have been in the gym at least three times this week
while these others have lingered over lunch
& yours are nowhere around as yet

is there a barstool around here somewhere
how do your shoulders feel after encountering hers

how the weather changes at our backs

the aching palm of the hand no sooner touches the chin
when suddenly there's a flurry of snow at the window

a breakfast scene at 6:00 with greasy hair
a mean sideburn interleaves
the shining layers of the surface of the globe

an aquiline nose or two never did anybody any harm
I reassure myself

such a delicate neck
eyebrows diminished to the point of oblivion
the further we got from the fields
the more it became a set piece face to match the day
a forehead like a rabbit brow in
version to the self

a blank erotic mouth sings the history of lack
as you ponderously scratch the left side of your neck
with your right hand

these others shriek attention
of an unseen crowd of
Rowlandson grotesques

the hennaed hair sways
to a thousand synthetic kisses

emerging from the pits
in a swirl of conviviality
white man turning grey against the stars the reds
blue neon spiral in
shiny blackstuff

you look into her eyes her teeth her chin
like a well-muscled dentist on vacation the hero
surrounded by her so-called friends
you look up you look down
she turns her hip upon the Li-lo

soaked in the smell of Ambre Solaire the heads move
to place the particle of food into your mouth
the finger the bratwurst
hesitation before nose installation

are you there mon ami

yes I'm scratching my chin

the bathers with their green & orange towels
running on the darkened beach
buttocks & nipples all aglow
the shadowy armpits

earlier in the day
sun burning in the pool
the well fed swimmers
tell each other things behind their hands

the way you stroke your nose
the way you swing off key
your hat your rod your staff descending

the finger extends from a green lip
& twirls a hat around the index

silent in court
& rank in the treads

this one holds his head in his hand
this one holds his hands akimbo
in readiness for whatever fate awaits him

as the fork the stick the bicycle wheel
contend the yellow
frieze along the lilac stairs

a collection of party hats
grieve over their departed innocents

auf der Mauer steht mit gelber Kreide

they want culture war
sidelong glances & the bland determined stare
a splendid neck-tie in the company of friends
transcends the category of ridiculous garment

what comfort in that tiny window
to pay the supreme penalty
his grey trouserless legs
swinging among the assembled heads

he who wrote it watches forever at the gate

o gorgeous neck-tie in das Meer
where the figures wait
to be towed away

a long violet glove
touches the painted lips with velvet

yucca yucca wonder bar
detachable collar & tie

back to the stone
back to the strong arms of the man you love

those looks of hers which measure the depths of something

you pass above the cloud of senses
you pass along the crowd of sense

like a chisel along a previously silent block of gritstone
pain is just the memory of a higher future or a severed past

the feathered dancer in the sky at night
tells me something behind the hand of the clock

the shadow in the frame of light from the projector
drinking Coke from a gleaming phantom

no contest Mr

then come what may
we'll eat today

& look at her & her
tomorrow

a gestural piece of lino escapes from another work

as you walk the neon night
in a flash of red

who smiles on you
above the rolling wheels of headlit cars

the heads in the cafe bars encroach upon your dreams
at dawn the lingering smile you never met
& never was the Laura of your dreams

the last touch of warmth at her breast before you left

I want to kiss your ochre lips
reach out for the curve at the top of your inner thigh

what aching countenance what loving smiles
what anxious caring eyes

offset by shaven napes
white turning grey over you

I say no to all your luxury
the greatest luxury of all

their heads attired in orange glories
refraining from absolute devastation
they do look down

tremble beneath that steady gaze
& rise to her turning away
to the faint sound of her bangled wrist
the darker side of you

feel a little cold the chink of light
prise open the lower edge of sky
at the tops of the concrete

miles & miles & miles away
the yellow stripe
as night surrenders to the dawn

above the empyrean
gyration of yellow dancers
pale shadows of our former selves
their looks are bigger than all of you

John I was only dancing
green electricity & rock
in the naked happiness of your loving arms

blue flashes lead us forward through the encircling gloom

& you are standing there in the gallery which is
after all is said & done a
very nice place to put pictures &
wondering about the creases & folds which inevitably appear
in your new corduroy trousers mere mortals
they fold you up like perfect movement

in the strategy of the brush the hand the arm
no more crossing out

the second crossing out supersedes the first crossing out
we bow in awe their heads look down
& measure the depths of something
they've got it taped the lines the angles the arrows
the unwritten rules they
don't take notes they are beyond gravity
they are the object of a loss of self-attention
body & fantastic solo runners gymnasts o danseuses
the long yellow beam of the spotlight
in the view from the gods
as the smoke curls up from the pit from the stalls
you smile in your solitude & isolation in the sky
washing the dust of each day's journey from your face

Local

the early morning sky across the lough
the very early light of day
a little cognac

a shining drop on the golden skin
mahogany amber chenille
table & curtain

swallow an olive

no it's not that autumn scene you love
the tiny clouds you've been attentive to
the lamplit comer of the roof

it's spring & a child in red smocking
walks unsteadily near the byre
her name is Róisin

pale as the early morning trees
a northern air
warms to the touch of sudden eyes

a seasonal delay

no longer falters at the margin
doorstep & window
work like a charm

the hand at ease at the white vellum
the rain soft in the hedgerow
dark & calm

drifting smoke as the coals are lit along the street
high walls a stone of steady grey
blue lustre of wet slate

curling o'er the flickering heart
a voice outside
the open path

soon it will be time enough to eat
a quiet beer
a slice of soda bread

back to the big room still as it was
a ready measure
for the level trace

the vast tumultuous heaven
off-white & blue
rears overhead

it does that a lot we take no notice
another tractor rolling by
in the big wide hills

a sunlit moment at your fingernail
a cup of milky tea
before it all shuts down again

or the evening breaks into a glow
a call to the bar
inviting dry but mellow

after the whirling passage of the sun
the silent company
at rest awhile now work is done

After Eugène Boudin

you abandon us
to swim in that full sky
to arrive at a fondness for cloud

the mass of their suspense
is moving from the depth of grey
to make it clear how blue the haze

Lines for Richard Long

somewhere in England in 1967
a line is made by walking in the green
& a window opens like a door on Clifton Down

those were the days as now
the south-west wind brings elevation of the broken cloud
dispelling the milky film of Cambridge habit
from the eastern sky a day for acoustic guitar

the touch of weather on these shiny roof-tops
is of no immediate importance or utility
the countless days the countless stones continue

all that language all that writing
indelible distance we travel us to

still holding the line still walking the line
at variable speeds not necessarily fast

a day a night forever all that making it
can say or do

& as the sun-wheel turns over Crickley
high into Monmouthshire

the spokes aflare
with a light dusting of lime

Turf Circle

a north wind moves over the winter sky-line

in opening cloud
the hesitation of the stars

an echo in the hollow

in the Bell Pool
the blue salmon

a clear leap to Usk

the walker rest
by the harbour wall
on the isle of Mona
that pleasant crossing-place

paddle & breaker
gull & wave

"oh pigling you were my sole companion in the forest

I walked from Kilconnell along the Cliffs of Moher & down into Fisherstreet & I came to the *Circle in Ireland* just as you said it was quite unchanged save for the flowers growing in the cracks on the flat fissured limestone beds above the sea & the Aran Islands below Connemara & the Twelve Pins across the bay to the north-west the power of The Burren away at the back the changing skies above & the Cliffs to the south

Later sailing into Cill Rónáin from Ros an Mhil I recognised the north-west landfall of Inishmaan & thought to look for the *Stones* toward the southernmost coast of Inishmore the following day. The next morning reading T. Robinson's map of the islands I found the work to be clearly indicated & so I walked out along to the old tower & down to the field of stones where many of yours still plainly stand pointing back across the Sound & through the islands back to the *Circle* & Clare

the grey colour of a pear
in the quiet light of the kitchen
the glittering branches at the window

the force of the hearth breaks out
invoking name & lineage

it's a good step
that will continue to the end without arriving

When you take up your pack & go
to the remote & desert places of the Earth
your path is a watercourse
or a torrent on the slope

the walker in summer-time on slanting ground
in a robe of vapour

by night there will be shelter
in the hollow & the cleft

I was a walker in earth before I was proficient in learning
catching the deep night & dawn divide
the line of the curling wave on the extended shore

now the leg thinks in distance & the arm in weight

CLOUD SUN CLOUD THUNDER CLOUD HAIL RAIN SUN

Saturday lime Sunday oak & quick-thorn
the place of the little drop & the length of the Avon
when it fills when it overflows
when it disappears in a dark thicket
quick sunlight between clouds

& from above the tops of the whirling trees
measure the veil of the drops in the air
at the width of the river's mouth
when the sea is turning round

the words in the book & the book in its beginning

Colonial Medley

valse moderato espressivo

the Wicklow hills are very hard
but to walk there again

before the young day shades to mist
the shining cliffs of Glenmalur

there's a tear in your eye
that should never be there at all

at all the power in your smile
the stones jump up beguiled

& if you go there's scarce a face
in these low lands that partly seems my own

when all is left a single chord
to break at night

oh sing sad harp
this sing for me

poverty

I used to think whenever my mother
called me Silent O'Moyle
he must have been a Newtown man

then I encounter Thomas Moore

New Road East

the amice the alb & the radio

Paul Robeson singing
Macushla Macushla

her white arms are reaching

catechism

penniless
for land or kine

I called on Napper Tandy
beside a ghostly barrow

the pale moon rose
above the shining wave

he sd
it wasn't like 1916 in 1916 either

mixed marriage medley

out of the sleeping west
that dangerous gap

came a dark bandage
it sd

discourse the darling
in sunshine or in shadow

but when you kiss
you're one of nothing

the little shirt me mother made for me

Danny

a little bit of shrapnel fell
from out the sky one day

the call to foreign parts
he'd thought to follow

it sd if your name is
Timothy

then I'm green turning red
over you

Grace

God bless us & save us
sys Anthony Davies

I never knew bloaters was fish

Also by John James

Mmm ... Ah Yes
The Welsh Poems
Trägheit
The Small Henderson Room
In One Side & Out the Other (with Andrew Crozier & Tom Phillips)
Letters from Sarah
Striking the Pavilion of Zero
A Theory of Poetry
War
Toasting
Berlin Return
Poem for Bruce McLean
Lines for Richard Long
The Ghost of Jimi Hendrix at Stokesay Castle
Local
Dreaming Flesh
Kinderlieder
Schlegel Eats a Bagel
Collected Poems
In Romsey Town
Cloud Breaking Sun
Songs in Midwinter for Franco
Sabots
On Reading J.H. Prynne's *Sub Songs* (with Bruce McLean)

Lightning Source UK Ltd.
Milton Keynes UK
UKHW03f1252290318
320233UK00002B/19/P